MISTAKES
THAT
WORKED

MISTAKES THAT WORKED

THE WORLD'S FAMILIAR INVENTIONS AND HOW THEY CAME TO BE

Charlotte Foltz Jones

Illustrated by John O'Brien

Delacorte Press

All rights reserved. Published in the United States by Delacorte Press,
an imprint of Random House Children's Books, a division of
Penguin Random House LLC, New York.

Originally published in different form by Doubleday Books for Young Readers,
an imprint of Random House Children's Books, a division of
Penguin Random House LLC, New York, in 1991.

Delacorte Press is a registered trademark and the colophon is a trademark
of Penguin Random House LLC.

randomhousekids.com

Educators and librarians, for a variety of teaching tools,
visit us at RHTeachersLibrarians.com

Library of Congress Cataloging-in-Publication Data
Names: Jones, Charlotte Foltz, author. | O'Brien, John, illustrator.
Title: Mistakes that worked : the world's familiar inventions and how
they came to be / Charlotte Foltz Jones ; illustrated by John O'Brien.
Description: [New edition] | New York : Delacorte Press, [2016]
"First edition." | Originally published: New York : Doubleday, 1991.
Identifiers: LCCN 2015049796 | ISBN 978-0-399-55202-1 (hc)
ISBN 978-0-399-55203-8 (ebook)
Subjects: LCSH: Inventions—Juvenile literature.
Classification: LCC T48 .J66 2016 | DDC 609—dc23

Printed in the United States of America
10 9 8 7 6 5 4 3
First Edition

Dedicated to Forrest Foltz
With special thanks to Bill Jones and John Jones

Acknowledgments

Bangor Chamber of Commerce

Ed Bartley, Dunkin' Donuts

Joan Beliveau, Dunkin' Donuts

Kathie Bellamy, Baskin-Robbins, USA

Barbara and Bill Brownlee, International Brick
    Collectors Association

Mary Cash

Donald A. Fischer, 3M

Claire Jackson, Coca-Cola USA

Betty M. James, James Industries

Patricia M. Jent, Procter & Gamble, Co.

Maxine C. Johnson, Scott Paper Co.

Edward Jones, Circus Historical Society

Peggy V. Jue, Levi Strauss & Co.

D'Ann King-Monroe, Tennessee State Library and Archives

Corinne Kirchner, American Foundation for the Blind

Leoma B. Maxwell, Avon Park Historical Society and Museum

Bill McCarthy, Circus World Museum

Sally Miller, Procter & Gamble Co.

Nestlé Foods

Neil Nix, Glenbrook Laboratories, Div. Sterling Drug

Nome Convention and Visitors Bureau

John Perduyn, Goodyear Tire & Rubber Co.

Potato Chip/Snack Food Association

Roy Renfrow, Malvern Chamber of Commerce

Anne Reynolds

Phil Rice

Marvene Riis, South Dakota Historical Society

Dan Roddick, Wham-O

Dean Rodenbough, Binney & Smith

Jim Russell, Popsicle Industries

B.E. Saffer, General Shale Museum of Ancient Brick

Lori Scholz, The Seeing Eye, Inc.

Harold Sloan

Rob Smelstor, VELCRO, USA

Lina Striglia, Binney & Smith

INTRODUCTION

Name the greatest of all the inventors. Accident.

—Mark Twain (Notebook)

C all them accidents. Call them mistakes. Even serendipity.

If the truth were known, we might be amazed by the number of great inventions and discoveries that were accidental, unplanned and unintentional.

The inventors mentioned in this book were not only smart but also alert. It is easy to fail and then abandon the whole idea. It's more difficult to fail but then recognize another use for the failure.

Much research and documentation has gone into each entry of this book, and some fun, interesting, and sometimes humorous stories about various discoveries emerged. Some of the stories are fact. Others are legends or lore—stories that can't be proved and probably can't be disproved.

The discoveries related in this book are just the beginning of ideas. Research, experimentation, and hard work were needed to develop the subjects into the products we use today.

The inventors and discoveries mentioned in this book should teach all of us the lesson stated best by Bertolt Brecht in 1930: "Intelligence is not to make no mistakes, but quickly to see how to make them good."

CONTENTS

CHAPTER 1

FAVORITE FOODS

Many cooks admit their favorite recipes were the result of accidents. But the numerous cases of food poisoning prove many food accidents don't work.

If you would like to experiment in the kitchen, a good book to start with is Vicki Cobb's *Science Experiments You Can Eat* (HarperCollins, New York). But be careful. The National Safety Council reports that almost eight hundred thousand victims of accidents involving home kitchen appliances and housewares are treated in hospital emergency rooms each year. So learn the safety rules and don't become a statistic.

KITCHEN SAFETY TIPS

✓ Ask permission from a parent or other adult before beginning any kitchen project.

✓ Always wash your hands before handling foods or cooking utensils.

✓ Read the recipe carefully and get out all ingredients and equipment before you begin.

✓ Follow the recipe exactly and measure accurately.

✓ Use electrical appliances only with an adult's supervision.

✓ When you are finished, put unused ingredients away and clean the kitchen. Never leave a mess.

Frozen Dinner Rolls

Baking rolls or bread from scratch is not quick.

The ingredients are mixed, then kneaded. The dough rises for up to two hours. Then it gets punched, divided into rolls, and baked for at least another hour.

Joe Gregor *knew* there must be an easier way for busy people to have hot rolls. He spent long hours trying to devise a method, but without success.

Then, one afternoon in 1949, Gregor was baking dinner rolls in his Avon Park, Florida, kitchen when the town's fire siren wailed. As a volunteer fireman, he had to respond to the fire. He quickly pulled his rolls from the oven and rushed out the door.

When he returned from the fire, Gregor examined the cold, half-cooked rolls. They were white and looked like plaster. Most people would have thrown the ugly mess in the garbage. But not Joe Gregor. He reheated his oven and finished cooking the rolls.

They were delicious! Gregor had accidentally discovered a method for making rolls ahead of time, yet serving them hot and fresh at the dinner table.

Gregor experimented to find the exact temperatures and times required for the first baking. He then revealed the directions to bakers everywhere.

Today, bakeries do the mixing, kneading, rising, and even part of the baking. Mr. or Ms. N. A. Hurry can buy frozen, partially cooked dinner rolls, heat them for ten minutes, and eat! . . . thanks to Joe Gregor and the Avon Park volunteer fire department.

Cheese

There he was: an ancient Arabian traveling across the desert with no one for company but a camel with yellow teeth, bad breath, and a bad temper.

At least the fellow had food along. He had poured some milk into a pouch made from a sheep's stomach. During his journey, he opened the pouch and discovered that the milk had separated and formed thick masses, which we call curd, and a watery fluid, which we call whey. The Arabian traveler had accidentally invented cheese.

Two elements had transformed milk into cheese: First, the sun had warmed the bag of milk during the journey. Second, the sheep-stomach bag contained dried digestive juices. The digestive juices included rennet, which is necessary to make cheese even today.

The Arabian traveler told his friends about his discovery, and for four thousand years, people have continued making cheese. Cheese quickly became important all over the world. Milk spoiled quickly, but by making cheese, people could preserve the milk's nutrition for long periods of time.

If you are an average American, you ate 33.7 pounds of cheese in 2013. That's what the National Cheese Institute estimates. According to the *International Dairy Federation,* while the United States is the largest producer of cheese, the average French person eats the most cheese—57 pounds each year.

Over two thousand varieties of cheese are produced around the world. If you tasted a different kind each week, it would take almost forty years to sample all the varieties. And by that time, someone would probably have developed some new ones to try, too.

FUN FACTS ABOUT CHEESE!

According to the *Guinness Book of World Records*, the largest cheese ever made was 40,060 pounds. It was made in 1988 in Wisconsin. A specially designed, refrigerated "cheese-mobile" moved the giant cheese from place to place.

The United States dairy industry sponsors National Dairy Month in June. It began as National Milk Month in 1937.

"Cheese" in other languages is:

French—*fromage*

Spanish—*queso*

Italian—*formaggio*

German—*Käse*

Polish—*ser*

Hungarian—*sajt*

Russian—*sir*

Japanese—*chiizu*

Swahili—*jibini*

Swedish—*ost*

Chocolate Chip Cookies

George Washington never tasted one.

Neither did Benjamin Franklin, Abraham Lincoln, or Mark Twain.

Unfortunately, they died before the chocolate chip cookie was invented.

Thanks to Ruth Wakefield, chocolate chip cookies were invented in 1938 and are available all over America today.

Wakefield did not plan to invent a cookie that would become the country's favorite. She was busy with the chores of running the Toll House Inn, located on the toll road between Boston and New Bedford, Massachusetts.

While mixing a batch of cookies, Wakefield discovered she was out of baker's chocolate. As a substitute, she broke some semisweet chocolate into small pieces and added them, intending to produce chocolate cookies.

When she removed the pan from the oven, Wakefield was surprised. The chocolate had not melted into the dough, and her cookies were not chocolate cookies. Wakefield had accidentally invented the chocolate chip cookie.

They were named Toll House Cookies after Ruth Wakefield's inn and are the most popular variety in America today. Estimates say seven billion chocolate chip cookies are consumed annually, and half the cookies baked in American homes are chocolate chip.

These popular treats have even provided full-time jobs; some vendors sell nothing but chocolate chip cookies.

They also made a political appearance in 1980. After Canadian diplomats assisted six American hostages to escape from Iran, the American people sent chocolate chip cookies to the Canadian embassy—our way of saying thanks.

If you would like to make chocolate chip cookies, the following recipe is furnished by Nestlé Foods for the original Toll House Cookies.

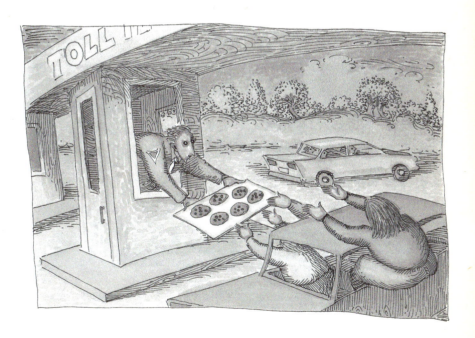

• Recipe •

TOLL HOUSE COOKIES

- 2¼ cups unsifted flour
- 1 teaspoon baking soda
- 1 teaspoon salt
- 1 cup butter, softened
- ¾ cup white sugar
- ¾ cup firmly packed brown sugar
- 1 teaspoon vanilla extract
- 2 eggs
- 1 twelve-ounce package (2 cups) Nestlé Semi-Sweet Chocolate Morsels
- 1 cup chopped nuts

Preheat oven to 375° F. In small bowl, combine flour, baking soda, and salt; set aside. In large bowl, combine butter, white sugar, brown sugar, and vanilla extract; beat until creamy. Beat in eggs. Gradually add flour mixture, mixing well. Stir in chocolate morsels and nuts. Drop rounded teaspoonfuls of dough onto ungreased cookie sheets.

Bake for 8 to 10 minutes.

Makes 100 two-inch cookies.

TOP TEN BESTSELLING COOKIES

1. Nabisco Oreo
2. Nabisco Chips Ahoy!
3. Nabisco Double Stuf Oreo
4. Pepperidge Farm Milano
5. Private label chocolate chip cookies
6. Little Debbie Nutty Bars
7. Little Debbie Oatmeal Creme Pies
8. Nabisco Chips Ahoy! Chewy
9. Nabisco Nilla Wafers
10. Private label sandwich cookies

Coca-Cola

The date was May 8, 1886.

The Civil War had been over for twenty-one years.

Grover Cleveland was president of the United States.

And in Atlanta, Georgia, a pharmacist named John Pemberton was busy in his backyard. Pemberton had already invented French Wine Coca—"The Ideal Nerve Tonic, Health Restorer and Stimulant," Lemon and Orange Elixir, and Dr. Pemberton's Indian Queen Magic

Hair Dye. But he wanted to invent a remedy for people who imbibed too much.

Using a boat oar to stir, Pemberton cooked up a mixture in a brass kettle heated over an open fire. When he finished, he had a new medicine to relieve exhaustion, aid the nervous, and soothe headaches.

Pemberton took his new medicine to the Jacobs Pharmacy. He instructed Venable, his assistant, to mix the syrup with water and chill it with ice. They tasted it and agreed it was delicious. But when Venable mixed another glass, he accidentally added carbonated water instead of plain water.

This time the men became excited. They decided that instead of offering the beverage as a headache remedy, they would sell it as a fountain drink—an alternative to ginger ale and root beer. They named it Coca-Cola after the coca leaves and cola nuts it contained.

In 1886, Coca-Cola sales averaged nine drinks a day. According to the Coca-Cola Company, Pemberton sold twenty-five gallons of syrup that first year. He took in $50 but spent $73.96 on advertising.

Today, nearly 10,450 soft drinks manufactured by Coca-Cola are consumed every second of every day, including Diet Coke, Fanta, and Sprite.

FUN FACTS
ABOUT COKE!

According to the Coca-Cola Company, if all the Coke ever produced were placed in twelve-ounce cans and stacked in single columns the height of Mount Everest, it would take nineteen million columns of cans to hold the Coke.

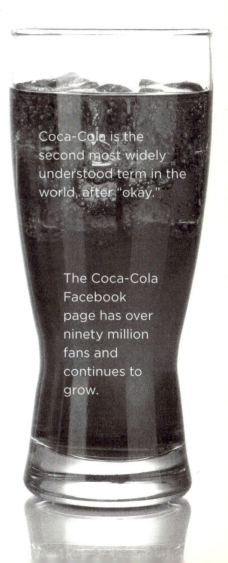

Coca-Cola is the second most widely understood term in the world, after "okay."

The Coca-Cola Facebook page has over ninety million fans and continues to grow.

Doughnut Holes

Hanson Gregory was born in 1832 in Camden, Maine, and died in 1921. He is buried in the Sailors' Snug Harbor Cemetery in Quincy, Massachusetts. During the eighty-nine years that Hanson Gregory lived, he spent many of them as a sea captain. A legend says he was at sea when he invented the doughnut hole.

One night he was eating a fried cake when a violent storm suddenly arose. Captain Gregory needed both hands to steer the ship, so he shoved the cake onto one of the spokes of the ship's helm to keep it safe. Without thinking, he invented the doughnut hole.

When Captain Gregory realized what he had invented, he was pleased. The centers of the fried cakes were always unpleasantly soggy, so removing the center definitely improved the cake. After the storm, the captain ordered the ship's cook to begin making fried cakes with a hole in the middle.

Another, less interesting story says that when Gregory was fifteen, he was watching his mother make fried cakes. Since he disliked the soggy centers, he simply suggested she remove them. Mrs. Gregory tried her son's idea and it worked.

Today, experts estimate that $11.6 billion worth of doughnut holes are sold each year. That's a lot of holes!

Fudge

One definition of the noun "fudge" is "nonsense or foolishness." And that's how our favorite chocolate candy got its name.

A story says that in the 1890s, a candymaker in Philadelphia was supervising his employees as they made caramels. Someone made a mistake, and instead of producing a chewy candy, the batch turned into a finely crystallized, nonchewy substance.

"Fudge!" the candymaker swore. And with that exclamation to describe the mistake, fudge was born.

Throughout the years, there have been many variations of fudge, but here is a simple recipe:

CREAM CHEESE FUDGE

Recipe

1 six-ounce package semisweet chocolate morsels
2 three-ounce packages cream cheese, softened
4 cups sifted confectioners' sugar
2 tablespoons evaporated milk
1½ teaspoons vanilla
¼ teaspoon salt
2 cups chopped nuts

Melt the chocolate morsels in the top of a double boiler. In a mixing bowl, beat cream cheese until smooth. To the cream cheese, add confectioners' sugar and evaporated milk, and blend. Stir the melted chocolate into the cheese mixture. Stir in the vanilla and salt, then the chopped nuts. Press mixture into a well-greased 9-inch-square pan. Cover and refrigerate overnight.

(Note: Cream Cheese Fudge is a modern recipe and *not* the original "mistake" recipe.)

Ice Cream Cone

The Chinese made iced desserts thousands of years ago, and George Washington was fond of ice cream, but the ice cream cone was not popular until after 1904.

Two food vendors had stands near each other at the 1904 World's Fair in St. Louis. Ernest A. Hamwi, a Syrian who had been in the United States a year, was selling zalabia. Zalabia was a wafer-thin Persian waffle. Nearby, another stand was selling ice cream.

Summer in St. Louis is h-o-t, and the ice cream vendor soon ran out of dishes in which to serve his ice cream. Hamwi quickly rolled one of his waffles into a cone shape and topped it with a scoop of the neighbor's ice cream. The treat was an instant hit and the "World's Fair Cornucopia" became what we know today as the ice cream cone.

While the story of Hamwi's ice cream cone is generally accepted, another man thought a lot like Hamwi. An Italian named Italo Marchiony ran a pushcart business in New York City selling lemon ice in a cone. At first he used a paper cone, then a pastry one.

Marchiony even applied for a patent in September 1903, and received it in December—six months before the St. Louis World's Fair began.

Great minds think alike! Both Hamwi and Marchiony devised the idea for an ice cream cone. But it was probably the large number of people who tasted Hamwi's cones at the St. Louis World's Fair that made the ice cream cone the popular treat we know today.

Hot fudge is the world's most popular ice cream topping.

Chocolate is the #1 flavor of ice cream in the United States.

It takes about fifty licks to finish a single-scoop ice cream cone.

California produces the most ice cream in America.

Maple Syrup

Warm days. Cool nights.

That's the magic formula for sugar maple tree growers. And February through March or April is the magic time to tap the trees. A single maple tree might give from ten to twenty-five gallons of sap.

The history of maple syrup goes back many centuries, and there is a legend about its discovery.

The story says Chief Woksis, an Iroquois, left camp in early March for a day of hunting. As he left, he pulled his tomahawk from the maple tree where he had hurled it the night before. During the day, sap dripped from the tree into a vessel standing close to the tree trunk.

When the evening came, the chief's wife noticed the

"tree water" (which we call sap) in the vessel. She decided to use the tree water to prepare supper and save herself a trip to the spring. As it cooked, the sap boiled down into a syrup. When Chief Woksis arrived home, he was delighted with the new maple flavor of his supper.

Native Americans called the sweetener maple water, and as early explorers and settlers arrived in North America, they taught the white man how to process maple syrup.

Modern technology has improved the sap-gathering process as well as the evaporation method. But no one can improve on the natural goodness of real maple syrup.

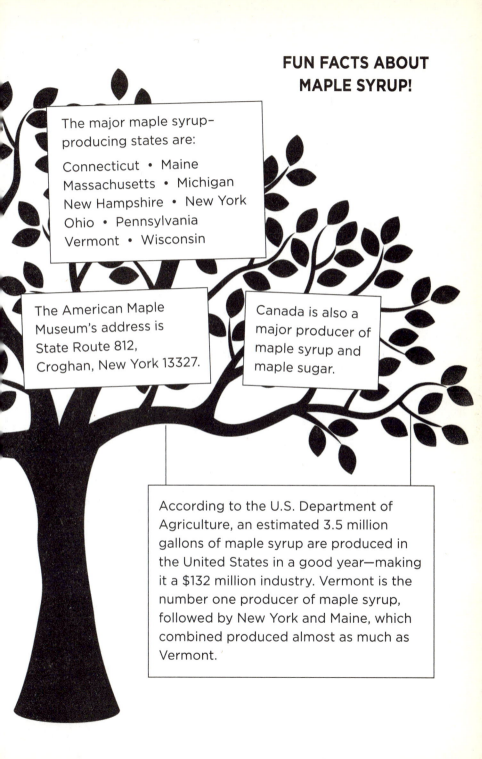

FUN FACTS ABOUT MAPLE SYRUP!

The major maple syrup–producing states are:

Connecticut • Maine
Massachusetts • Michigan
New Hampshire • New York
Ohio • Pennsylvania
Vermont • Wisconsin

The American Maple Museum's address is State Route 812, Croghan, New York 13327.

Canada is also a major producer of maple syrup and maple sugar.

According to the U.S. Department of Agriculture, an estimated 3.5 million gallons of maple syrup are produced in the United States in a good year—making it a $132 million industry. Vermont is the number one producer of maple syrup, followed by New York and Maine, which combined produced almost as much as Vermont.

Popsicles

On September 7, 1975, the Westside Assembly of God Church in Davenport, Iowa, made a huge ice pop. The *Guinness Book of World Records* lists their 5,750-pound creation as the largest iced lollipop on a stick. The frozen treat might have been big, but it wasn't a genuine Popsicle, since Popsicle is a registered trademark name and is made under a patented formula.

Popsicles were actually invented in 1905 by eleven-year-old Frank Epperson of California—and the invention was accidental.

One day, Frank mixed some soda-water powder with

water, which was a popular drink in those days. He left the mixture on the back porch overnight with his stirring stick in it. The temperature dropped to a record low that night, and the next day, Frank Epperson had a stick of frozen soda water to show his friends at school.

Eighteen years later—in 1923—Frank remembered his frozen soda-water mixture and began a business producing Epsicles in seven fruit flavors. The name was later changed to Popsicle.

One estimate says that more than two billion Popsicle frozen treats are sold each year. There are more than twenty-five different flavors to choose from, but Popsicle's owner says the general favorite through the years has been cherry.

Potato Chips

Americans spend almost $7 billion every year on a treat we know as potato chips. A popular story says they were invented in 1853 in Saratoga Springs, New York. Many wealthy people vacationed at Cary Moon's Lake House in Saratoga Springs, and a Native American chef named George Crum worked in the kitchen there.

One day, a customer kept sending his plate of fried potatoes back to the kitchen, asking that they be sliced thinner and fried longer. George Crum had a bad temper, and he decided to get even with the complaining diner. He sliced the potatoes very thin, fried them till they were curly crisps, and salted them. Certain the guest would hate them, he had the potatoes delivered to the table. To everyone's surprise, the patron was delighted and asked for more.

Word spread quickly of these crispy potatoes, and until the early 1900s, they were known as Saratoga chips after the town where they were introduced.

Today, over 30 billion pounds of potato chips are consumed in the United States each year. A total 3,468 billion pounds of potatoes end up as America's number one snack food: potato chips.

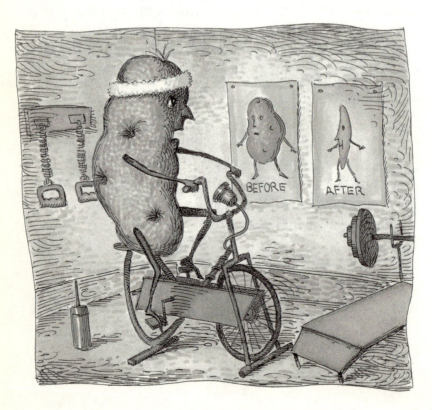

FUN FACTS ABOUT POTATO CHIPS!

- The ordinary, unruffled potato chip is 55/1000 of an inch thick.

- Of the total United States potato crop, 11 percent becomes potato chips.

- Charles Chip, Inc., is listed in the *Guinness Book of World Records* as producing the largest potato chip. Displayed in February 1977, it was four inches by seven inches.

- Potato chips are now available in assorted varieties, such as:

  cajun
  jalapeño
  sour cream and onion
  Italian
  yogurt
  barbecue
  cheese
  cheese with bacon

  and even chocolate-covered!

- About eleven million pounds of potato chips are eaten on Super Bowl Sunday alone.

Sandwiches

The year was 1762.

In America, the Revolutionary War had not yet started, and George Washington was not yet president.

In Europe, six-year-old Wolfgang Amadeus Mozart began touring as a child prodigy.

But in England, John Montagu, 4th Earl of Sandwich, was busy gambling. One day he had been at the gaming table for twenty-four hours and didn't want to take time out to eat. When the servants brought his food, he ordered the meat served between slices of bread so he could eat and still keep one hand free to control his bets.

And that's how he invented . . . the sandwich.

Bread's history goes back at least thirty thousand years, so people had probably eaten sandwiches before. But once they were given a famous name, sandwiches became one of the most popular meals eaten in the Western Hemisphere. One estimate says three hundred million sandwiches are eaten every day in America.

FUN FACTS ABOUT SANDWICHES!

John Montagu was born November 3, 1718, so November 3 is National Sandwich Day.

Towns in Illinois and Massachusetts are named Sandwich.

When Captain James Cook discovered the Hawaiian Islands in 1778, he named them the Sandwich Islands in honor of John Montagu.

Americans eat more than three hundred million sandwiches every day—an amazing statistic, since there are slightly more than three hundred million Americans.

The most popular sandwich in America is turkey, followed by ham as a close second.

The average American will have consumed 1,500 PB&Js by the time he or she graduates from high school.

Tea

What kind of world would this be without tea?

There would be no teapot or teakettle if tea had never been discovered. There would be no teacup, teaspoon, or tea towel, and no teatime.

Two of the world's most famous parties would have been canceled: The colonists could not have held the Boston Tea Party in 1773 and thrown 342 chests of tea into Boston Harbor. And Lewis Carroll's *Alice's Adventures in Wonderland* would say nothing of the March Hare's tea party.

Luckily, tea was discovered in 2737 BC by a great Chinese emperor named Shen Nung.

One day, Shen Nung was boiling water outdoors when leaves from a nearby bush fell into the open kettle.

Before Shen Hung could retrieve the leaves, they began to brew. He smelled the sweet aroma of the mixture, and once he tasted it, the world was given tea!

Tea is the most popular beverage in the world today—after plain water. It was introduced in Europe in 1610, and until about two hundred years ago, people in many Asian countries used blocks or bricks of tea as money.

One estimate says that more than four million metric tons of tea are consumed worldwide each year. That means the people on planet Earth drink about a trillion cups of tea a year. That's a lot of tea!

FUN FACTS ABOUT TEA!

Thirty-five percent of the world's tea comes from China.

A town in South Dakota is named Tea.

Around the world, *tea* is:

French—*thé*
Spanish—*té*
Turkish—*cay*
Russian—*cháy*
Arabic—*shaye*
Japanese—*cha*

Tea Bags

Thomas Sullivan invented tea bags, although he did not realize it at the time. Sullivan, an American coffee and tea merchant, often sent samples of his products to his customers. The samples were packed in cans. One day in 1904, Sullivan decided it would be simpler and less expensive to send the samples in small, hand-sewn silk bags.

Soon the orders began arriving, but surprisingly, they were not for his tea. The orders were for tea packaged in little bags. The customers had discovered the small bags made tea brewing easier.

Tea bags have been improved over the years, and today, over half the tea consumed in American homes is made from them.

CHAPTER 2

DOCTOR, DOCTOR

Louis Pasteur, the famous French chemist
and bacteriologist, told his students in 1854,
"Where observation is concerned, chance
favors only the prepared mind."

Aspirin

For thousands of years, doctors told patients suffering from pain to chew on the bark of a willow tree. Even as far back as 400 BC, Hippocrates recommended a tea made from willow leaves.

It wasn't until the 1800s that scientists discovered what was in the willow tree that relieved pain and reduced fever. The substance was named salicylic acid. But when people suffering from pain took the salicylic acid, it caused severe stomach and mouth irritation.

In 1853, a thirty-seven-year-old French chemist

named Charles Gerhardt mixed another chemical with the acid and produced good results, but the procedure was difficult and took a lot of time. Gerhardt decided the new compound wasn't practical, so he set it aside.

Forty-one years later, Felix Hoffmann, a German chemist at Bayer & Co., was searching for something to relieve his father's arthritis. He studied Gerhardt's experiments and "rediscovered" salicylic acid, which he combined with acetic acid to make acetylsalicylic acid—or aspirin, as we know it.

Charles Gerhardt had mistakenly thought his compound was not useful, but today one hundred billion aspirin tablets are produced and sold annually all over the world.

Scientists are still finding new uses for aspirin. Researchers hope it will prevent heart attacks and strokes, slow the growth of cataracts and cancerous tumors, and help manage diabetes.

However, aspirin is not recommended for people under the age of sixteen because of its suspected connection to the potentially fatal Reye's syndrome.

Aspirin is one of America's most widely used drugs. And the little white tablet is certainly easier to carry in a pocket than the willow tree is!

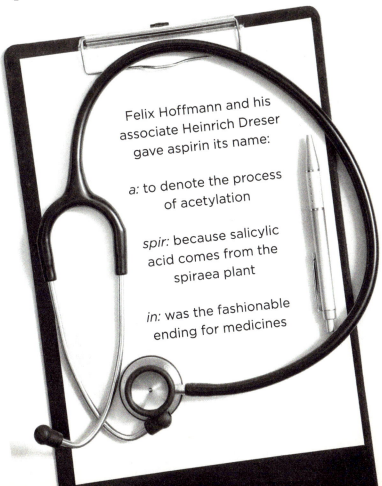

Felix Hoffmann and his associate Heinrich Dreser gave aspirin its name:

a: to denote the process of acetylation

spir: because salicylic acid comes from the spiraea plant

in: was the fashionable ending for medicines

Seeing Eye Dogs

World War I lasted more than four years—from 1914 to 1918. During that time, approximately 8.5 million people were killed and 21 million were wounded.

Near the end of World War I, a doctor was walking outside a German military hospital with a soldier who had been blinded in battle. The doctor's dog joined the walk and when the doctor was called into one of the buildings, the blind solider was left alone with the dog.

Soon the doctor returned, but the blind man and the dog were missing. When the doctor found them, he discovered the dog had led the blind patient across the hospital grounds.

The doctor was amazed by what his untrained pet dog had done and decided to see how well a trained working breed of dog could lead a blind person. The results were so good that a dog guide program was established in Potsdam.

An American woman named Dorothy Eustis visited Potsdam to learn about the dog guide program. And through an article she wrote for the *Saturday Evening Post,* she brought the program to public attention in the United States. The first American dog guide school, The Seeing Eye, was established in 1929. Today, seventeen major U.S. organizations train dogs and instruct blind people in their use.

The most popular breeds are German shepherds, golden retrievers, and Labrador retrievers. They must learn hand gestures and simple commands in order to lead the blind person across streets and around people, obstacles, holes, and low-hanging awnings or tree limbs.

The dog must also learn to exercise good judgment. If the blind person gives a "forward" command but the dog sees danger, the dog must know when to disobey. This is called intelligent disobedience.

Dogs guiding blind masters is not new. Wall paintings, ancient scrolls, and legends tell of dogs leading blind men since 100 BC. But until the German soldier was led by the doctor's untrained dog, and the first training program was initiated, the incidents were scattered and the dogs were not always efficient.

In the case of dog guides, the old saying is true: a dog really is a man's—or a woman's—best friend.

According to the American Foundation for the Blind, about seven thousand blind persons in the United States use dog guides.

Penicillin

Alexander Fleming didn't get out of bed one September morning in 1928 planning to invent penicillin. But that's exactly what he did.

Fleming, then forty-seven years old, was a bacteriologist, a scientist who studies germs. He was experimenting in his laboratory at St. Mary's Hospital in London, England, and had set aside some petri dishes containing staphylococci bacteria, intending to clean them later. When he returned to the dishes, he discovered that one was contaminated with a mold.

Many people would have thrown it away, but Fleming reexamined the dish. Under his microscope, he saw that the staphylococci around the edges of the invading

mold had been destroyed. But the staph colonies farther away were still there. The deadly staphylococci were actually being dissolved by the mold.

Through the accident of the moldy culture, Alexander Fleming gave the world penicillin.

Howard Florey, Ernst Chain, Norman Heatley, and other researchers at England's Oxford University experimented with Fleming's discovery and successfully developed penicillin into the lifesaving drug that is used all over the world today.

In 1945, Fleming, Florey, and Chain were awarded the Nobel Prize in Medicine for their discovery and perfection of penicillin.

Today, penicillin has affected almost every family in the developed nations.

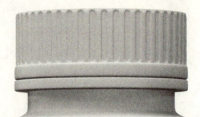

Andrew J. Moyer was inducted into the National Inventors Hall of Fame in 1987 for his Patents 2,442,141 and 2,443,989. Moyer's discovery of how to make penicillin in large quantities has saved millions of lives and prevented untold suffering from infectious diseases.

X-Rays

X-ray machines are located in almost every hospital, dentist's office, and clinic in America. They are even in airport terminals, where you can watch airport officials x-ray carry-on luggage.

Credit for the invention of X-rays goes to Wilhelm C.

Roentgen, who died in 1923. Roentgen was a German physicist and professor at the University of Würzburg. On November 8, 1895, he was working in his laboratory with a Crookes tube, a vacuum tube that produced streams of weak electrons called cathode rays. While experimenting in a darkened room with cathode rays and an electric current, he noticed that a fluorescent screen three or four feet away glowed. He was amazed since the Crookes tube was surrounded by black paper that prevented ordinary light from escaping. A popular story says he discovered the rays' penetrating power when he realized he had unknowingly photographed a key that was inside a book.

Roentgen continued his experiments with the new invisible rays, and named them X-rays since they were an unknown type of radiation. Later, some scientists called them Roentgen rays. Roentgen was awarded the Nobel Prize in Physics in 1901 for his discovery of X-rays.

The U.S. Food and Drug Administration reports that seven out of ten Americans receive a medical or dental X-ray each year. But more than just a medical discovery, X-rays are also used in astronomy, chemical analysis, and industry.

FUN FACTS ABOUT X-RAYS!

A person who receives too many X-rays risks getting cancer, leukemia, cataracts, burns, or other health problems. Pregnant women are advised to avoid X-rays, and all people should request that a lead apron be used to shield their eyes and reproductive organs during an X-ray.

The measure of doses of radiation produced by X-rays is called a rad, a rem, or a roentgen.

Radio waves vary in length from twelve inches to larger than planet Earth. Visible light waves have lengths of 308 to 700 nanometers. X-rays have very small wavelengths, some no bigger than a single atom of many elements.

CHAPTER 3

FUN, FUN, FUN

Someone once said, "Failure is the
battle scar of someone who tried." But
success can be that battle scar, too!

The Frisbee

The Frisbee was invented 2,700 years ago!

Well . . . not really!

Discus throwing was a part of the early Olympic games in Greece 2,700 years ago. And the design of the Frisbee disc is similar to the discus thrown in the Olympic games. But the Frisbee is a Frisbee, not a discus. And its invention was *not* the result of some inventor staying up nights.

The original Frisbee was spelled Frisbie, and it was metal. It was not invented to be thrown—except into an oven. It was a pie tin stamped with the words "Frisbie's Pies" because the pies came from the Frisbie Pie Company in Bridgeport, Connecticut.

The Frisbie pie tins would probably have done nothing more than hold pies if it hadn't been for some Yale University students. The Yale students bought Frisbie pies, and once the pies were eaten, they began tossing the tins to one another. They would call out "Frisbie!" to the person to whom they were tossing a pan, or to warn people walking nearby to watch for the flying objects.

And so, intending simply to toss a pie tin back and forth, the Yale University students invented the use for what has grown into the Frisbee we know today.

Walter F. Morrison produced the first plastic model. The Wham-O Manufacturing Company of San Gabriel, California, began manufacturing Frisbee discs in the 1950s; since 1957, it has made sixteen models.

There are Frisbee clubs, tournaments, champions, a world association, and a publication just for Frisbee enthusiasts. The National Air and Space Frisbee Festival is held each September.

Guinness World Records reports that the record Frisbee distance was set by Simon Lizotte on October 25, 2014, with an 863.5-foot throw.

Disc play is good exercise. It's fun. It's easy, yet challenging. It doesn't cost much. And best of all, it's a sport you can enjoy with your favorite dog!

Piggy Bank

Dogs bury bones.

Squirrels gather nuts to last through the winter.

Camels store food and water so they can travel many days across deserts.

But do pigs save anything? No! Pigs save nothing. They bury nothing. They store nothing.

So why do we save our coins in a piggy bank? The answer: because someone made a mistake.

During the Middle Ages, in about the fifteenth century, metal was expensive and seldom used for household wares. Instead, dishes and pots were made of an economical clay called pygg.

Whenever housewives could save an extra coin, they dropped it into one of their clay jars. They called this their pygg bank or their pyggy bank.

Over the next two hundred to three hundred years, people forgot that "pygg" referred to the earthenware material. In the nineteenth century, when English potters received requests for pyggy banks, they produced banks shaped like a pig. Of course, the pigs appealed to the customers and delighted children.

Pigs are still one of the most popular forms of coin banks sold in gift shops today.

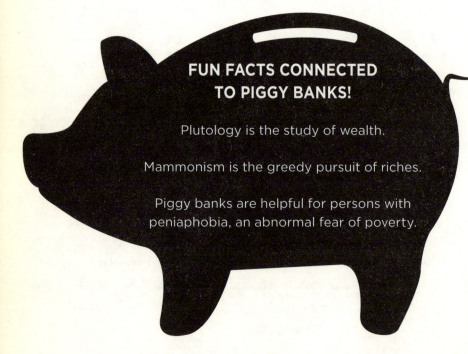

FUN FACTS CONNECTED TO PIGGY BANKS!

Plutology is the study of wealth.

Mammonism is the greedy pursuit of riches.

Piggy banks are helpful for persons with peniaphobia, an abnormal fear of poverty.

Silly Putty

Sand.

There's lots of sand on planet Earth. In fact, there's tons of it.

From sand, chemists can refine silicon. Plenty of silicon.

During World War II, the United States government needed a synthetic rubber for airplane tires, soldiers' boots, and other uses. Since silicon was so widely available, the government asked several large companies to have their engineers try to make a rubber substitute out of silicon.

In 1944 at General Electric, one of the engineers working on the silicon experiments was James Wright. One day while he was doing tests with silicon oil, he added boric acid. The result was a gooey substance that bounced.

Unfortunately, it had no apparent use. Samples were sent to engineers all over the world, but no one could find a use for it.

Then, in 1949, four years after the war ended, a man named Peter Hodgson had an idea. After borrowing $147, he encased the goo in plastic "eggs" and renamed it Silly Putty. Then he began selling it as a toy, first to adults and several years later to children.

It stretches. It bounces. When whacked with a hammer, it shatters. It if is pressed against newspaper comics, it will pick up the imprint. Silly Putty is truly amazing. It is now over fifty years old, and was one of the most popular "fad" toys in mid-twentieth-century America.

It has been used by athletes to strengthen their hand and forearm muscles. It can level the leg of a wiggly table or clean typewriter keys. It removes lint from clothes and animal hair from furniture.

The astronauts on the *Apollo 8* spacecraft played with Silly Putty when they got bored, and they used it to keep tools from floating around after they left Earth's gravity.

It was used by the Columbus Zoo in Ohio in 1981 to take hand- and footprints of gorillas.

It's the toy with only one moving part, and best of all, Silly Putty is still priced so that everyone can afford it.

Slinky

In 1943, during World War II, an engineer in the United States Navy was on a new ship's trial run. As he worked, a torsion spring suddenly fell to the floor. The spring flip-flopped as the ingenious man watched.

The naval engineer's name was Richard James, and when he returned home, he remembered the spring and the interesting way it flip-flopped. James and his wife, Betty, perfected a long steel ribbon tightly coiled into a spiral. They began production in 1945.

From the torsion spring's accidental fall came a toy Americans have enjoyed for seventy years: the Slinky.

The nonelectrical, no-battery-required, nonvideo toy has fascinated three generations of children and adults alike. According to one estimate, more than 350 million Slinkys have been sold, and the only change in the original design has been to crimp the ends as a safety measure.

The Slinky is still hopping, skipping, jumping, and bouncing across floors and down stairs all over America.

CHAPTER 4

ALL KINDS OF
ACCIDENTAL THINGS

William E. Gladstone once said,
"No man ever became great or good except
through many and great mistakes."

In 1875, the director of the United States Patent Office quit his job and suggested that his department be closed. There was nothing left to invent, he insisted.

Someone once asked, If necessity is the mother of invention, why does so much unnecessary stuff get invented? Among the more unusual patents granted in the United States are:

a propeller-driven rocking chair
an automatic spaghetti-spinning fork
a power-operated pool cue stick
a baby-patting machine
an electronic snore depressor

a parakeet diaper

an alarm clock that squirts the sleeper's face

Every year, invention conventions are held all over the United States and online. Organizers of the annual INPEX invention show near Pittsburgh say its purpose is to "showcase inventors and present an inventor-of-the-year award." And there is now an Invention Convention for kids at the Hagley Museum and Library in Wilmington, Delaware.

Bricks

In New York City, the Empire State Building was constructed with over ten million bricks.

The Great Wall of China stretches fifteen hundred miles and contains almost four billion bricks.

Bricks have been used for nine thousand to ten thousand years, making them the oldest man-made building material.

Some archaeologists believe that the first bricks were made by accident. They were probably formed when mud or silt was deposited by the Nile River in Egypt. After the mud hardened into slabs, the slabs cracked. When an Egyptian walking along the Nile saw the slabs, he realized they could be shaped into blocks and used for building.

Some of the ancient bricks that have been found are as strong as the bricks manufactured today. The method of making bricks is still almost the same. Clay is mined, crushed, and mixed with water. The thick goo is then shaped, dried, and baked. Machines have made the crushing and mixing processes easier. Large ovens have replaced the sun drying. But the basic procedure has changed very little.

Brick plants are built near clay deposits suitable for making bricks. One site is near the town of Malvern, Arkansas. Total production there is 150 million bricks a year—so many that Malvern calls itself the Brick Capital of the World. The town celebrates each year with a Brickfest.

Many people even collect bricks. Their organization is called the International Brick Collectors Association. There, adults as well as children from the United States, Canada, Great Britain, New Zealand, and Australia share their interest in bricks. But they don't collect just any brick. They collect bricks that have names or markings on them.

Anyone interested in old bricks can visit General Shale's Museum of Ancient Brick, 3015 Bristol Highway, Johnson City, Tennessee 37601. Among many fascinating bricks, a visitor can see:

◆ The oldest sun-dried brick ever found. It is from beneath the biblical city of Jericho. Experts estimate it is between nine thousand and ten thousand years old.

- ◆ The oldest fired brick ever found. It was discovered at Kalibangan, India, and is five thousand years old.
- ◆ A sixty-four-pound brick from a fortress of King Solomon.

This museum is free and open during standard business hours.

Glass

Bullets can bounce off it. Noise can shatter it. You can

see through it or see yourself in it. It has gone into the oven, to the bottom of the ocean, and to the moon.

But we'll probably never know exactly who invented glass or when the process for making it was discovered. Perhaps workers noticed glass that accidentally resulted from a manufacturing process using fire.

Pliny the Elder, a first-century Roman writer, claims Phoenician sailors accidentally invented glass. He suggests the sailors were camping on the shores of Palestine and brought ashore two blocks of natron (carbonate of soda) from their ship's cargo. They used the blocks to support their cooking pots over the fire where they were camped. The fire caused the natron and the beach sand to melt together and create glass.

Historians know glass has been used for at least six thousand years. Egyptians were one of the first people to make glass on a large scale. Solid glass beads (usually blue!) have been found in Egyptian ruins dating before 2000 BC.

While the basic process for making glass has not changed, modern technology has improved the procedure and the quality.

Glassblowing

The art of glassblowing was not invented until about the first century BC, when a glassmaker's tube accidentally closed on one end. To remove the blob of glass, the glassmaker blew into the tube from the open end. Instead of opening up, the blob became a bubble—and the artisan had unintentionally invented glassblowing.

While the same principle is still used for glassblowing today, modern machines have improved its efficiency. A machine can blow approximately two thousand lightbulbs in one minute—quite an improvement over the methods used two thousand years ago.

Safety Glass

One day in 1903, Edouard Benedictus, a French chemist, accidentally knocked a glass flask to the floor of his laboratory. The glass shattered, but when Benedictus glanced down, he was amazed that the broken pieces still hung together in the shape of the flask.

Benedictus discovered that cellulose nitrate, a type of liquid plastic, had been stored in the flask but had evaporated. After the flask broke, the glass fragments had clung to the strong plastic film that had formed on the inside of the flask.

Soon after his discovery, Benedictus read a newspaper article about automobile accidents in Paris and the many injuries caused by broken windshield glass. Benedictus knew his nitrocellulose-coated glass had a practical use.

Automobile manufacturers, however, wanted to keep the cost of cars down and weren't interested in using

such expensive glass. Besides, they installed safety measures only to prevent accidents—not to prevent injury.

When World War I started in 1914, manufacturers used Benedictus's safety glass for gas mask lenses. Soon after the war was over, safety glass had proven itself in military battles, so automobile companies began using it for car windshields.

FUN FACTS ABOUT GLASS!

According to Guinness World Records, the thinnest glass is only two atoms thick. It was accidentally discovered in 2012 by researchers at Cornell University and Germany's University of Ulm.

The Corning Museum of Glass is located at One Museum Way, Corning, New York 14830. There is an admission charge.

Crystallophobia is the abnormal fear of glass.

"Glass" in other languages is:

French—*verre*
Italian—*vetro*
Russian—*stekló*
Japanese—*garasu*
German—*Glas*
Turkish—*cam*
Arabic—*zougag*
Swahili—*kioo*

Ivory Soap

Ivory Soap is 99 and 44/100 percent pure . . . and IT FLOATS!

Did it take years of experimenting to get that soap to float?

Not exactly. Ivory Soap floated by accident.

Two brothers, James and David Gamble, were partners in the Procter & Gamble Company, which manufactured soap. For four years, they had been developing a formula for a high-quality soap at an affordable price.

In January 1878, the brothers finally perfected the formula. They called it simply White Soap and began production.

Several months later, the accident occurred.

As one story goes, a large batch of White Soap was mixing when a workman at the factory went to lunch and left the machinery running. When he returned, he found that air had been worked into the mixture. He decided not to discard the batch of soap because of such a small error, and he poured the soap into the frames. The soap hardened and it was cut, packaged, and shipped.

A few weeks later, letters began arriving at Procter & Gamble, asking for more of the soap that floated. The workman's error had turned into a selling point!

Harley Procter came up with the name Ivory while listening to a Bible reading one morning in 1879.

Ivory Soap is over a hundred years old and still 99 44/100 percent pure. But best of all, it still floats!

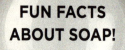

FUN FACTS ABOUT SOAP!

If Ivory Soap is 99 44/100 percent pure, what's in it that is 56/100 percent impure? Here's Harley Procter's answer:

uncombined alkali 0.11%
carbonates 0.28%
mineral matter 0.17%

Approximately forty billion cakes of Ivory Soap have been manufactured to date.

Paper Towels

The Chinese invented paper about two thousand years ago, but it wasn't until the mid-1800s that paper was made from wood pulp. After the discovery of this method, almost anything was made of paper:

clothes
boats
watches
horseshoes
outhouses
a church
chimneys
barrels
railroad wheels and rails
skating-rink floors
false noses
bathtubs
coffins
a piano
washtubs
house insulation

And, of course, bathroom tissue (otherwise known as toilet paper).

In the early 1900s, Scott Paper Company, a large

distributor of bathroom tissue, routinely purchased large rolls of tissue paper for converting into bathroom tissue.

In 1907, one of the company's paper suppliers sent a shipment of paper that had too much wrinkling and was too heavy. Arthur Scott didn't return the paper to the manufacturer. Although it was unsuitable for bathroom tissue, he knew it could be used.

He perforated the paper so it could be dispensed in individual sheets. He called the sheets Sani-Towels and sold them to railroad stations, hotels, schools, and business and industrial buildings. In 1931, he made the disposable towels available to American homes.

Today, they come in "decorator colors" or "country designs." Some are big and tough; others are strong and absorbent. Some are soft, others, economical.

But the paper towels we use today are the result of a paper manufacturer's mistake.

Post-It Notes

By now, everyone knows what Post-it brand notes are: they are those great little self-stick notepapers.

Most people have Post-it Notes. Most people use them. Most people love them.

But Post-it Notes were not a planned product. No one got the idea and then stayed up nights to invent it.

A man named Spencer Silver was working in the 3M research laboratories in 1970, trying to find a strong adhesive. Silver developed a new adhesive, but it was even weaker than what 3M already manufactured. It stuck to objects but could easily be lifted off. It was superweak instead of superstrong.

No one knew what to do with the stuff, but Silver didn't discard it.

Then one Sunday, four years later, a 3M scientist named Arthur Fry was singing in his church choir. He used paper markers to keep his place in the hymnal, but they kept falling out of the book.

Remembering Silver's adhesive, Fry used some to coat his markers.

Success! With the weak adhesive, the markers stayed in place, yet lifted off without damaging the pages.

In 1980, 3M began distributing Post-it Notes nationwide—ten years after Silver developed the super-weak adhesive. Today, they are one of the most popular office products available.

Vulcanization of Rubber

Tires.

Shoe Soles.

Baby bottle nipples.

Artificial cow hearts.

These and hundreds of other things are made of rubber.

Rubber is the tree sap that puts the bounce in a basketball, keeps river water out of fishermen's hip boots, and rolled a rock-collecting cart across the moon.

But rubber isn't a new discovery. An ancient pictograph shows figures bouncing little rubber balls, and on Christopher Columbus's second trip to the New World, he saw boys playing with balls made from the hardened juice of a tree.

In 1770, Joseph Priestley, an English scientist, found that the gum of the tree rubbed out his writing mistakes. With that fantastic discovery, it was named rubber.

Like Central and South American natives, as well as Spanish and Portuguese explorers, the American rubber industry made crude shoes and waterproofed clothing with the milky liquid of the wild rubber tree. But hot weather melted the substance, later named latex, into a gooey, smelly mess. And in cold weather, the rubber turned brittle and shattered like glass. By the mid-nineteenth century, the rubber industry was near collapse.

To try to make rubber stable and dependable, a man named Charles Goodyear tried mixing it with magnesium, turpentine, alcohol, slaked lime, nitric acid, and finally sulfur. Then one day in early 1839 in Woburn, Massachusetts, Goodyear accidentally dropped a glob of his rubber-sulfur mixture onto a hot kitchen stove. As he scraped up the mess, he realized the stove's intense heat had made the rubber firm and flexible. He tested it outside in the frigid winter air. The next morning, the rubber was not brittle.

Goodyear had succeeded. He named the heating process vulcanization after Vulcan, the Roman god of fire.

In his autobiography, Charles Goodyear admitted the discovery was not the result of "scientific investigation." He wrote that he "carelessly brought [the mixture] in contact with a hot stove."

Because of Goodyear's determination—and an accident—rubber is one of the world's major industries. Goodyear was inducted into the National Inventors Hall of Fame in 1976 for his invention of the vulcanization process. But the discovery didn't make Charles Goodyear a rich man. When he died in 1860, he was two hundred thousand dollars in debt.

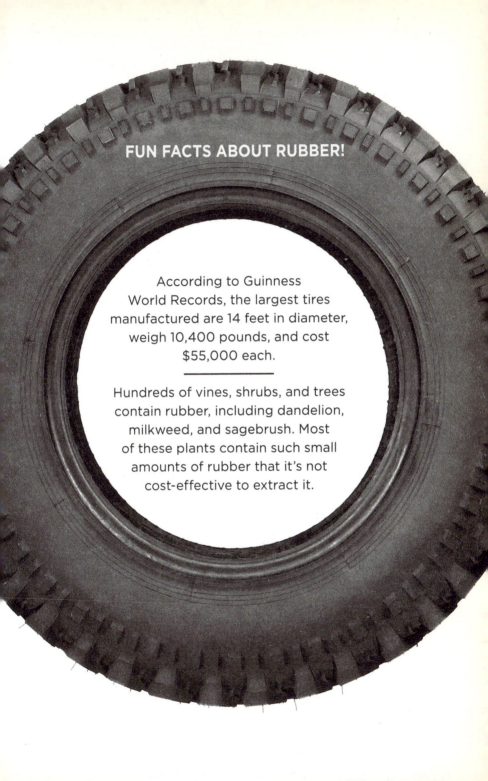

FUN FACTS ABOUT RUBBER!

According to Guinness World Records, the largest tires manufactured are 14 feet in diameter, weigh 10,400 pounds, and cost $55,000 each.

Hundreds of vines, shrubs, and trees contain rubber, including dandelion, milkweed, and sagebrush. Most of these plants contain such small amounts of rubber that it's not cost-effective to extract it.

CHAPTER 5

WHAT THEY WEAR

Only he who does nothing makes a mistake.
—French proverb

Cinderella's Glass Slipper

Everyone knows Cinderella. She's the famous fairy-tale star.

Poor Cinderella had to stay home and work while her stepsisters attended the Prince's ball. But Cinderella's Fairy Godmother suddenly appeared and transformed Cinderella's ragged clothes into a gown. The Fairy Godmother warned Cinderella that she had to leave the ball by midnight because her gown would turn back to rags at that hour.

Cinderella had a wonderful time at the ball and forgot

the warning until the clock began to strike midnight. In her hurry to leave, Cinderella lost one of her glass slippers.

The Prince had fallen in love with Cinderella and searched for the maiden who could wear the slipper. When he found Cinderella, they married and lived happily ever after.

This fairy tale probably began in China. Over five hundred versions of Cinderella have been told in Europe alone. The version most of us know came from Charles Perrault's 1697 book, *Mother Goose's Tales.* And that is where a mistake was made.

In earlier versions, Cinderella's slippers were made of fur. *Vair* is an old French word that means a type of fur. *Verre,* which is pronounced the same as *vair,* means "glass."

It is believed that when Charles Perrault wrote the French version of Cinderella more than three hundred years ago, he confused *vair* for *verre.* And poor Cinderella has had to wear glass slippers ever since.

Velcro

For thousands of years, humans have walked through fields of weeds and arrived home with burrs, a rough covering of a nut or seed, stuck to their clothing. It's amazing no one took advantage of the problem until 1948.

George de Mestral, a Swiss engineer, returned from a walk one day in 1948 and found some cockleburs clinging to his cloth jacket. When de Mestral loosened them, he examined one under his microscope. The principle was simple. The cocklebur is a maze of thin strands with burrs, or hooks, on the ends that cling to fabrics or animal fur.

By the accident of the cockleburs sticking to his jacket, George de Mestral recognized the potential for a practical new fastener. It took eight years to experiment, develop, and perfect the invention, which consists of two strips of nylon fabric. One strip contains thousands of small hooks. The other strip contains small loops. When the two strips are pressed together, they form a strong bond.

Hook-and-loop fastener is what we call it today. Velcro, the name de Mestral gave his product, is the brand most people in the United States know. It is strong, easily separated, lightweight, durable, and washable; comes in a variety of colors; and won't jam.

There are thousands of uses for hook-and-loop fasteners—on clothing, shoes, watchbands, or backpacks; around the house or garage; in automobiles, aircraft, parachutes, space suits, or space shuttles; to secure blood pressure cuffs and artificial heart chambers. The list is never-ending.

The only bad thing about hook-and-loop fasteners is the competition they give the snap, zipper, button, and shoelace industries!

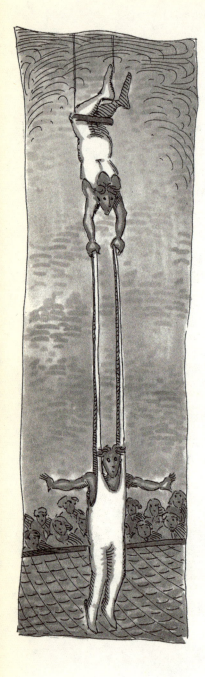

Leotards

The dictionary says a leotard is "a close-fitting one-piece garment." Leotards are sometimes called tights, and they are usually worn by gymnasts, acrobats, and dancers.

According to legend, Jules Léotard gave his name to the garment we now know as the leotard, but he didn't invent it.

A man named Nelson Hower was a bareback rider in the Buckley and Wicks circus in 1828. One day, Hower's costume did not come back from the cleaners, so he performed his act wearing his long underwear.

Other performers adapted the tight-fitting garments to their acts, but it took Jules Léotard to give it the name we know today.

Léotard, a French wire-walker and trapeze artist, began performing in Paris in 1859. He was the first acrobat to use a moving trapeze instead of a stationary bar. A song, "The Daring Young Man on the Flying Trapeze," was written about him.

Most people performing circus acts wore colorful, eye-catching costumes, but Jules Léotard chose the one-piece, tight-fitting garment. His performances were so outstanding that his name—and the "leotard" he wore—became famous.

FUN FACTS ABOUT LEOTARDS!

Today, one of the most well-known persons to wear leotards is Superman!

Visit the Circus World Museum, 550 Water Street, Baraboo, Wisconsin 53913, and the Ringling Circus Museum, 5401 Bay Shore Road, Sarasota, Florida 34243.

Levi's Jeans

The invention of men's pants was certainly no accident.

And Levi Strauss's success at making what we now know as blue jeans was no accident either.

However, Levi Strauss did not leave New York in 1853 hoping to become the biggest and most successful blue jeans manufacturer in the world. He didn't even intend to manufacture blue jeans.

Levi Strauss went to San Francisco in 1853 intending to sell dry goods. The California Gold Rush of 1849 had attracted thousands of prospectors, and Levi planned to sell canvas for tents and Conestoga wagon covers. But as Levi talked to the prospectors, they told him, "Shoulda brought pants. Pants don't wear worth a hoot in the diggin's!" So Levi had a tailor make some pants from his brown canvas. Word quickly spread about the quality of "those pants of Levi's," or simply "Levi's jeans."

When his supply of canvas was gone, Levi switched to another sturdy fabric, made in Nîmes, France. It was called *serge de Nîmes* (now known as denim). Levi improved his pants—changing the color to a deep blue and adding arcuate (arched) stitching and rivets to the pockets to prevent the weight of the gold nuggets from ripping them.

Levi Strauss's pants are still worn all over the world, and in 1976, a pair of Levi's jeans were put on display at

the Smithsonian Institution in Washington, DC, as part of the permanent collections in the National Museum of American History.

FUN FACTS ABOUT JEANS!

Why do we call them jeans? "Gene" was a form of the word "Genoese," meaning "from Genoa, Italy." In the late 1500s, sailors' pants were made of a cotton twill fabric made in Genoa. Those pants were often called genes, which was later changed to jeans.

The average American college student owns five to six pairs of jeans.

Each year, 1.2 billion pairs of jeans are sold around the world.

Trouser Cuffs

A story is told about the beginning of the cuff on men's trousers—that little roll-up on the pants leg near the ankle.

Supposedly, a large, formal wedding was being held in New York in the 1890s. A very fashionable Englishman was invited, but on the way to the church, he was caught in a rainstorm. The man did not want to spoil his trousers, so he quickly rolled up the bottoms to keep them from getting wet.

Because of the storm, the Englishman was late, and as he hurried into the church, he forgot to roll his pants legs down again.

Other guests noticed the rolled-up trousers but didn't realize there was a real, practical reason for the cuffs. They thought the turnup was the latest in men's fashion.

The cuff quickly caught on in America, and quite by accident, the Englishman started a style that still recurs every few years in men's fashion.

THE NATIONAL INVENTORS HALL OF FAME

The National Inventors Hall of Fame was begun in 1973. According to the United States Patent and Trademark Office, the hall of fame is "dedicated to honoring legendary inventors whose innovations and entrepreneurial endeavors have changed the world."

Three things qualify a nominee for induction:
- holder of a United States patent
- the extent to which the invention promotes the progress of science and the useful arts
- the contribution the invention has made to the nation's welfare

On National Inventors Day in February, the Patent and Trademark Office in Arlington, Virginia, honors inventors selected to be inducted.

MORE FUN FACTS!

Thomas A. Edison was the first Hall of Fame inductee in 1973. (He received 1,093 patents during his lifetime.) There are now more than five hundred inductees.

The public is invited to visit the National Inventors Hall of Fame. There is no admission charge and it is open during regular business hours.

It is located at the United States Patent and Trademark Office, 600 Dulany Street, Madison Building, Alexandria, Virginia 22314.

There is a display for each inventor, containing a brief description of his or her invention and an artifact connected with it.

Selected Bibliography

The Amazing Story of Aspirin. London: Aspirin Foundation, 1981.

Arizona Farm Bureau. *Fill Your Plate* (blog). "A Passion for Popsicles: 13 Fun Facts," August 26, 2011. http://fillyourplate .org/blog/a-passion-for-popsicles-13-fun-facts.

Arizona Farm Bureau. *Fill Your Plate* (blog). "6 Fun Facts about the Sandwich," October 26, 2012. http://fillyourplate.org/blog/6 -fun-facts-about-sandwiches.

Bergman, Peter M. *The Concise Dictionary of 26 Languages.* New American Library. New York: Signet, 1968.

Brasch, R. *How Did It Begin?* New York: David McKay, 1965.

Carter, Gordon. *Willing Walkers: The Story of Dogs for the Blind.* New York: Abelard-Schuman, 1965.

"Cinderella." *Encyclopedia Britannica*, Vol. 3, 1986.

Clendinen, Barbara. "Avon Park Man Invents Brown and Serve Rolls," *Tampa Morning Tribune,* December 30, 1949, C4.

Conjecture Corporation. "How Much Do Americans Spend on Potato Chips?" Accessed July 2015. wisegeek.com/how-much -do-americans-spend-on-potato-chips.htm.

Crockett, Zachary. "The Invention of the Slinky." *Priceonomics*, December 3, 2014. Accessed July 2015. http://priceonomics .com/the-invention-of-the-slinky/.

Culture magazine, Laurel Miller, Thalassa Skinner, and Ming Tsai. *Cheese for Dummies.* Mississauga, ON: John Wiley & Sons Canada, 2012.

"A Delicious Collection of Chocolate Chip Cookie Recipes." Accessed July 2015. best-ever-cookie-collection.com/chocolate -chip-cookie-recipes.html.

D'Estaing, Valérie-Anne Giscard. *The World Almanac Book of Inventions.* New York: Pharos Books, 1985.

Facts/Things of Interest—Silly Putty. Easton, PA: Binney & Smith.

Goodyear Tire and Rubber. *Charles Goodyear: 1800–1860.* Akron, OH: Goodyear Tire and Rubber Co. https://corporate.goodyear

.com/en-US/about/history/charles-goodyear-story.html.

Guide Dogs for the Blind. "Frequently Asked Questions (FAQ)."
Accessed July 2015. http://www.guidedogs.com/site
/PageServer?pagename = about_overview_faq.

Hiskey, Daven. "Post-It Notes Were Invented by Accident." *Today
I Found Out*, November 9, 2011. Accessed July 2015. http://
www.todayifoundout.com/index.php/2011/11/post-it-notes
-were-invented-by-accident/.

International Aspirin Foundation. "History of Aspirin." Accessed
July 2015. aspirin-foundation.com/history-of-aspirin.

"In the Spirit of Ivory," Cincinnati, OH: Procter & Gamble. "Ivory
Soap—Celebrating 100 Years as America's Favorite." Special
edition of *Moonbeams,* P&G employee magazine, 1979, p. 3.

Jacobs, Francine. *Breakthrough: The True Story of Penicillin.* New
York: Dodd, Mead, 1985.

Körner, Manfred. "German Tea Market: Hot Stuff, High Margins."
Tea & Coffee Trade Journal, July/August 2005. Accessed July
2015. teaandcoffee.net/0705/tea.htm.

Levi Strauss & Co. *Everyone Knows His First Name.* San Francisco:
Levi Strauss & Co., 1986.

Liedtke, Michael. *"How the Frisbee Got Its Name." New York Times,*
June 17, 2007.

"The Man Who Made a Million (with Something Nobody Wanted),"
Sunday Herald, March 12, 1961.

Maple Syrup Production. United States Department of Agriculture
National Agricultural Statistics Service, June 11, 2014.
Accessed July 2015. http://www.nass.usda.gov/Statistics_by_
State/New_England_includes/Publications/0605mpl.pdf.

McGrath, Molly Wade. *Top Sellers, USA.* New York: William
Morrow, 1983.

McWhirter, Norris, ed. *Guinness Book of World Records, 1988.* New
York: Sterling Publishing, 1987.

McWhirter, Norris, ed. *Guinness Book of World Records, 1989.* New
York: Sterling Publishing, 1988.

The Miracle of Rubber. Akron, OH: Goodyear Tire and Rubber Co.,
1984.

National Inventors Hall of Fame, Alexandria, VA. Accessed July 2015. http://invent.org/hall-of-fame.

Nearing, Helen and Scott. *The Maple Sugar Book.* New York: Schocken Books, 1970.

Polley, Jane, and Peter Chaitin, eds. *Stories Behind Everyday Things.* Pleasantville, NY: Reader's Digest, 1980.

Popsicle—A Part of American History. Englewood, NJ: Popsicle Industries, 1973.

Potato Chip/Snack Food Association. "Potato Chips Rocketing Ahead." *Snack Food Management Report.* Alexandria, VA: PC/SFA, July 1985.

Putnam, Peter Brock. *Love in the Lead: The Miracle of the Seeing Eye Dog.* New York: Dutton, 1979.

Refreshing Facts About Coca-Cola. Atlanta, GA: Coca-Cola Co., June 1987.

Sashin, Daphne, and Toby Lyles. "Blue Jeans Celebrate 140 Years." CNN, May 20, 2013. Accessed July 2015. cnn.com/2013/05/20/living/blue-jeans-history-irpt/index.html.

Scott: The Story of Paper Towels. Philadelphia: Scott Paper Co.

Smith, David C. *History of Papermaking in the United States (1691–1961).* New York: Lockwood Publishing, 1971.

Société des Produits Nestlé S.A. Ice Cream.com. HDIP, Inc.

"The Straight Scoop on Ice Cream." Accessed July 2015. icecream.com/icecreaminfo.

Suddath, Claire. "A Brief History of: Velcro." *Time* magazine, June 15, 2010. Accessed July 2015. content.time.com/time/nation/article/0,8599,1996883,00.html.

The Versatile VELCRO Fastener and The VELCRO Fastener Way. Manchester, NH: VELCRO, USA, 1983.

Watters, Pat. *Coca-Cola: An Illustrated History.* Garden City, NY: Doubleday, 1978.

Zettler, Howard G. *–Ologies & –Isms: A Thematic Dictionary.* Detroit: Gale Research, 1978.

Index